"He makes my feet like the feet of deer; he causes me to stand on the heights"

PSALM 18:33 (NIV)

About the Author

CoFounder of Lionheart Ministry, Carrie is a daughter of the King, a sinner daily in need of His grace, running after His presence. She is blessed with her beloved husband and two precious children. Her greatest joy is dancing with words of wonder and planting them onto pages with the Lord. Carrie's heart aims to serve God's people with His rich love, and is praying and yearning for a revival to sweep over His church.

For more writing and to order hardcover books online visit Lionheartministry.com

About the Songwriter

Lindsey is an artist, singer-songwriter, and journalist. She is the founder of Alabaster Heart, a ministry aiming to equip generations with worship and revival for the Lord's glory. She graduated from Pepperdine University in the Spring of 2021 and currently resides in Southwest Florida where she serves as a worship leader and music teacher for Lionheart Ministry and continues to pursue the Lord daily with her life, her love and her gift of song.

Connect with Lindsey at alabasterheart.co

About the Illustrator

Lynne resides in Queensland, Australia, and has been a professional artist for over forty years. Lynne teaches art classes and paints private commissions, including illustrating Christian books and media. God-inspired and Holy Spirit saturated, she paints the poetic promises of His heart on a canvas of hope. Lynne paints the promises of God radiantly displaying artwork from on high. Lynne thanks her heavenly Father for the privilege of co-creating art with Him.

Connect with Lynne at lynnehudson.com

About the Designer

Kayla is an entrepreneur, creative spirit, graduate of Liberty University, freelance Graphic Designer, and Wedding Photographer. Kayla has a heart for ministry and for using the creative talents that God has given her to provide biblical resources to people across the world. She finds her passion in bringing others' God-sized visions to life through design. Kayla looks to the Lord for guidance and wisdom each day; thanking Him for the opportunities, lessons, and lockstep journey that He is leading her on.

Connect with Kayla at kaylafollin.com

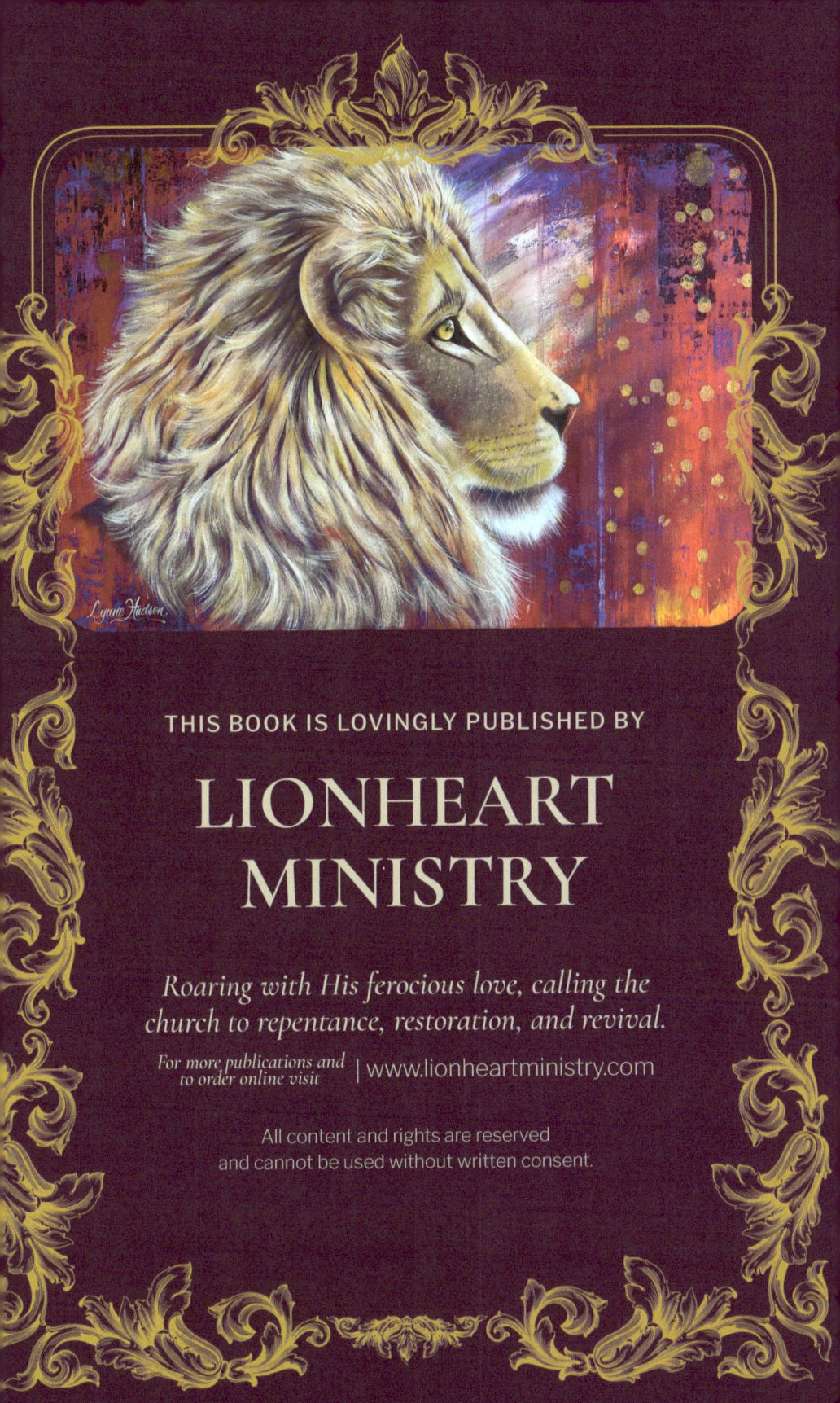

Run run run
little one

Run into a mountain
of kindness.

Jump over the
hills of rebellion

Cross over the sinking
swamps of shame.

Navigate through the waters
of turbulent opposition!

Crush the heads of the
venemous snakes
with the Gospel on your feet.

Crusade through the
dark forest without
fearing evil,

Using your staff of His
righteousness
to crush the temptations
of the wicked.

Provoke others to do good deeds, *honoring Him* by rushing through the thorns of regret.

Enter into *streams* of His mercy.

Bask in the waterfalls of *His deliverance*.

Wander through the *roaring cascades* of the mountainous glory of the Lord.

Lost lies cannot live where you are found in *Christ*.

Meander into flower fields and there you will *dance before the Lord* declaring a victory shout, *a bellowed laughter* with the Lord for taking you on a *journey of heights*.

It will be there you will
round up His *strength*
and be bolstered with
His *courage* as you run
toward the mountain of
heights.

You will be wounded on
your *climb up,*
for the arrows will try to
pierce you to death
through persecution.

But as you travel in His
Holy Spirit
shoes you will explore the
wonder + beauty
of the Lord.

There, up the mountain He
has allowed you to run,
shouting deliverances
for the near and the far.

Revival echoes from
your heartbeat of
exuding strength.

Your accuser becomes silenced because he can't *bear* to hear anymore praises reign

His voice is *muffled* by the praises of God's people upholding you on this journey.

Deep *calls* to deep, and you can hear the *roaring ocean* beyond the cliff of the mountain.

You are almost there, *heaving + laboring* in the work of the Lord with many following after you.

The trek was impossible and deadly but your God of the *miraculous* has sought to bring you forward.

Heights of Heaven await you.

Rising up, with every act of faith and courage, *you arrive*.

There, on that
mountain of valor, you are
clothed in confidence
as God's voice pierces
through blazing glory fires!

Shekinah glory fires are all
around you on the
mountain
of beauty!

There you can see
the kingdoms being
overtaken by God
through your obedience
and *unrelenting* faith.

You have *hearkened* to His call and He has saved cities from their rebellion, and now He is sending *revival fires* spreading like rapid fire over the lands.

Dominions of the adversary are burned by revivals!

Revelation 12:11 (NIV)
"They *triumphed* over him by the blood of the Lamb and by the *word* of their testimony; they did not love their lives so much as to *shrink from death*."

Dear Reader,

I pray you would hear the Father's song of love over you as you listen to this song. I pray that every note, every chord, and every lyric would minister to you and pull you deeper into His presence. For in His presence is the fullness of joy, and at His right hand are pleasures forevermore (Psalm 16:11). Enter into His heavenly flower fields, filled with the riches of His handiwork. Replenish your soul in the streams of His sweet delight and feel the refreshing wind of His spirit breathing on you from His holy hills. His very breath is filling you with the courage you need to walk out the path He has prepared for you. Set your feet to dance before Him. Precious child, the victory is secured in Him! Do you feel His fatherly delight in you? Lift your spiritual eyes to see the reality of His love before you. He is more real than any of our temporal circumstances in this life. Honor Him by being obedient to the journey He has set before you, and remember He is with you in all things. His spirit is faithfully and tenderly bringing you to Himself, by His spirit, through your journey of faith.

Scan the QR code to listen!

Lyrics:

Take a moment to take it in
Past to present, my handprint in everything
It's just a second, but it's gone before you blink
So don't cling to this life, my child
Come up here with me

Enter into flower fields
Streams of sweet delight, wind on holy hills
Cast your every care in my loving hands
Angels all around, set your feet to dance

Set your feet to dance
Lift your eyes to see
I am all around
Nothing in between

Set your feet to dance
Lift your eyes to see
Fill the atmosphere
With shouts of victory

Enter into flower fields
Streams of sweet delight, wind on holy hills
Cast your every care in my loving hands
Angels all around, set your feet to dance!

My Victory Voyage

My feet have finally landed on a rock of refuge after a long and perilous voyage of danger, suffering and pain. I petitioned with the Lord not once, but twice to avoid all costs of suffering, and stay in the comfortable secret place nestled on a mountaintop, but my Lord had other plans for sanctification and denied my request. You see, Romans 5 says:

> Therefore, since we have been justified through faith, we have peace with God through our Lord Jesus Christ, through whom we have gained access by faith into this grace in which we now stand. And we boast in the hope of the glory of God. Not only so, but we also glory in our sufferings, because we know that suffering produces perseverance; perseverance, character; and character, hope. And hope does not put us

to shame, because God's love has been poured out into our hearts through the Holy Spirit, who has been given to us. (Romans 5:1-5 NIV)

This is where my story begins but it is not where it ends!

First He ushered me into the doom of a desert. From the desert into a boat. From a boat onto a battlefield. From the battlefield into a cave and then from the cave up a mountain. It was a perilous journey, equipped by God to gain the victory by grace and through faith.

My story begins in the raging heat of the desert. I can't even begin to understand the complexity of the paths it took to get there. One turn led to another path and so forth. Even so, now I know — I was led by the Lord.

Drenched in sweat, my throat aching with thirst, my lips parched and cracked, with beads of sweat dripping down my back. Isolated and alone, I pray. I wasn't really alone but there were no people present in the flesh. My God, in whom I trust, promised to never leave nor forsake me. I could still feel the power of His presence with me, in me and around me but it was void of any human interference. The only sounds were those of the nighttime displays of His glory, with animals creeping and crawling about, filling the air with the constant cries and calls of the wild deep in the drought of the desert. How I had gotten here, I didn't know. Fear and fret intimidated my faith as the wind wailed, and the sand struck my face with force. 40 nights and 40 days. God placed me here, I reminded myself. Stories from scripture undergirded my faith as I remembered when Jesus entered His desert and fought Satan through fasting and truth.

Would I, and could I make it through? I anxiously pondered. Here in these depths of the travailing desert were hidden treasures, all provisional miracles from my Father! One by one, my Father released them. Manna came when I was hungry through an agave plant that appeared out of nowhere and an aloe plant quenched my thirst.

And there, in midst of the isolation, was the exact armor I needed provided to me, to prepare for the battle at hand. God gave me a sword, a spear, and head-to-toe attire to put on. Here in this place, the enemy spewed lie after lie to me. For 40 days I wrestled with the temptations of the forces of hell. Until I fought with the truth. Once I grabbed a hold of truth as my sword, I could fight my way through it, overcoming the attempts of the enemy. Through years of Bible memory, like wildfire the Spirit brought to mind scripture after scripture to fight and refute every last attack.

After 40 long days and 40 exhausting nights, I walked away weary but equipped to go on.

Beyond the sweltering heat of the desert, the Lord spoke, "Get into the boat."

As I looked to my left, there bobbing up and down, anchored in the sand was a boat of rescue. I inched forward into the muck and miry waters of trial. Drenched up to my knees, I frantically grabbed hold of my faith boat. I could hear a stampede. What was that noise coming from behind?

Engulfed in alarm, I looked behind to see armies pursuing me, soldiers of all shapes and sizes carrying large spears. They were shouting with accusations. An army of evil was rushing toward me like the speed of light, coming after the core of my heart, attempting to steal, kill and destroy what the Lord had just deposited deep within me from the desert.

They were so close! I screamed, "Abba Father!"

My body slammed into the tiny vessel, banging against the ground. I grabbed the ors and rowed with all my strength. The coolness of the deep sea splashed upon my face, salty waves rolled down my cheeks. I trembled with fear, my mind muddled with angst. I didn't even have a chance to call for help. My Abba knew of my distress.

Suddenly the Lord parted the waters, like a miracle invading earth with mighty ferocious love. Love came down and engulfed all the opposition behind me, swallowing them up whole. The accusations were silenced and immediately I shrieked in amazement. Like glass, the waters returned to calm, still and silent. Still and silent.

A rushing wind surfaced and the little decrepit boat I was in by faith could not survive in even the smallest of lakes, let alone this turbulent ocean. But faith took me sailing and so I surrendered. On a ship, a voyage of faith, a story of long suffering. I sailed away into the pounding seas of sorrows, with my Father holding my hand. His constant reassuring voice led me onward. A triumphant wind gust led me, gliding me this way and that way, taking ownership over the course of direction. The boat wobbled but my soul was content. Over my head flew a gleeful white bird; a dove, I pondered. In its beak it held an olive leaf. The dove gently let go of the olive leaf and it landed on my head ever so carefully. I quickly held onto my ticket of promise as Noah had experienced hundreds of years ago. A promise. My sobs of gratitude were smitten with the tenderness of God's love, shown by His miraculous hand. As the wind blew and the waves rocked the tiny boat up and down, up and down, He shushed me to sleep like a baby ministered to by a mother's lullaby. I nestled my weary head into a wooden nook of the barren boat and slumbered into a quiet place of sleep. I closed my eyes and thanked my loving Lord for His faithful protection. As I fell asleep at once, I dreamt of a refuge, an island oasis, a paradise, could it be heaven? I didn't know, but all I felt were surges of peace sustaining my rest!

Then suddenly I was awoken to a loud thud. I had hit land. Water splashed into the boat. This wasn't just any good old land! This was a battlefield. Shots rang through the air. I saw uneven grounds, trenches being built and bombs exploding everywhere. I turned my head from side to side in astonishment and fear, taking it all in.

As I stared in bewilderment, I heard my Father yell, "It's time! You're going to need to pick up the pace and run to the shelter beyond the fighting!"

I stumbled out of desperation with pure survival instincts rushing through my veins. "You're going to need to grab the weapons I've prepared you with," yelled the Lord.

Arrows and fiery darts zipped past me left and right, brushing against my armor. How would I survive a war like this? Thoughts of doubt invaded and tempted my carnal mind. Out of the tyranny of my thoughts, my Commander's voice interrupted and became louder as I ran.

"Shoot with my promises!" He commanded.

I understood the Commander's seriousness and concern in His voice and took my arrows of truth with my hands shaking. I chose to launch them wildly into the hills of my foes. Doubts began to dissipate and fear lost its hold on me in a blazing instant.

Amazed, I yelled to my Father, "What is that sound?"

All the way from heaven I could hear declarative drums beating to the sound of heaven's army! Each drum beat was symbolic of another place to put my moving feet. War drums cascaded the sky as the Lord battled with confidence and authority over my enemies.

I turned the corner and I heard the cheering care of my Commander say, "Now I'm hiding you in the cleft of a rock."

Behind the hidden ravine was the shelter He promised me. I arrived in the knick of time. The cave was covered with large vines, masking it as a hill beneath the growth of the leaves. I heard a large bomb explode behind me as my feet reached the cold wet ground of the cave. Courageously I made my way into the lingering intimidating darkness. My hands stretched into the open crisp air. One step at a time, I made it to the center.

The Lord said, "You've made it. Now rest."

On my aching knees, I wailed in prayer in the darkened cave, wondering how long I would be stuck in this darkness! How long could I survive all of these deadly terrains, obstacles and wars? How long could I be a soldier resting assured of victory when one battle led to another? My tears reminded me of my thirst, and my stomach cried out for sustenance. Before I could even muster up the energy to pray, a raven flew in, its wings flapping above my head. It dove an inch away from the top of my scalp, and the wind of its wings startled me. I was afraid it would bury itself and tangle into my hair. But as I peered a bit closer, I saw it was delivering Kingdom provisions. Tucked into its claws was meat and bread! My Father had sent another messenger bird to provide all of my needs! I hungrily ate, meditating on the faithfulness of God and letting the wonder and mystery of His promises fill my mind with hope.

Suddenly I heard angels singing. They sounded like a symphony. "Glory and honor, praise and power, unto our King, unto our King." They belted heavenly tunes unimaginable. It was a foreign language, that of angels, and yet I was given spiritual access and ability to hear. The tunes of triumph echoed in the darkness of the cave. I fell asleep on the cold damp floor that night, soothed, fed, and protected, listening to the choir of angels.

Light slowly peered in through the dark crevices and cracks of the cave. Outside I could hear the echo of the birds awakening a new day with a song, as if saying "Mercy, mercy, mercy."

My Abba Father whispered, "It is time, my child." I stumbled to my feet, sore but oddly not afraid.

He led me onward and out toward the end. There really was light at the end of the tunnel. The beaming light of the sun pierced hope into my heart as my eyes adjusted to the brightness of the rising day. I looked beyond and saw a tall, rugged, dangerous mountain. "How would I ever be able to climb that, Father?" I asked.

"Resist fear, and have faith," said my Father with reassuring love.

Higher and higher I climbed up the mysterious mountain. "One more step," He whispered. One more step."

Up the mountain I went, up a little higher. I could feel a spiritual strengthening deep within my soul, increasing through every faith-filled movement. The holy Word of God encircled my mind, chasing down the wolves of lies that tried to whine and wail to create fear. Courageous movements of my mind led to functional steps of faith. Led forth in love by my Father, trusting and entrusting myself to a faithful Creator every step of the way.

1 Peter 4:19 rang in my ears, "So then, those who suffer according to God's will should commit themselves to their faithful Creator and continue to do good." (NIV)

Once again, earthly hunger pounced on me like a vicious hound. My frail legs began to buckle. Physically I was empty. Suddenly, a belted kingfisher bird swept over my head, and his song seemed to sing "Jehovah Jireh, Jehovah Jireh."

"The Lord is my provider," I whispered. Miracles from the air mirrored the rhythm of rain, beating on the path with repetition. Thin flakes lined my path. "Miraculous mountaintop manna from the sky?" I exclaimed out loud, shouting to God.

My shouts reverberated so loud that I'm sure I awoke the mountain lions! With excitement I reveled that food and delivery from angels had really fallen from the sky like raining love.

"You give me more than I need!" I yelled. "You have provided for me, my Lord."

I quickly scarfed down some of the most edifying eternal breads marked by a miracle. My body nourished, my soul fed, I was equipped and ready to complete this voyage.

When I reached the top of the mountain, it was nearly nightfall. Owls began to coo, and other nocturnal animals left their posts with hunting as their lot. The day had passed by swiftly as I climbed the highest, most dangerous peak of the mountain. A finality, a finish line. When I reached the tip top peak, I stood on the only bed of a rock that I saw. Out of breath and winded from the strenuous climb, I inhaled and exhaled to catch my breath. I stretched my arms out wide in deep moments of surrender. It felt impossible to hold up the weight of my arms after the grueling journey but my mind retraced thoughts of Moses' mountain story and his own turbulent travels to the hills of transfiguration.

Bewildered, belabored and weary from the travels, I whispered grateful praises, "God, Emmanuel was with me on this deadly, impossible path. With God all things are possible."

My eyes felt heavy. But when I opened them I could see a heavenly sight of angels on every side of the mountain. This was the army that followed me from the desert, into the boat, to the war, into the cave and now carried me up the mountains. God assigned each angelic being, with an operational duty, a high calling to protect me.

As I stood upon the refuge rock, I glanced down to marvel at some sort of miraculous illumination. To my dismay, I was staring at a rock of glory under my feet on the highest part of the mountain. It glistened and shined in a dubious display of the Lord's overflowing, iridescent mercy. Words were written everywhere on this bedrock of stone. I gazed into the beams of hope-filled words and attributes of God engraved on the rock. Trust, power, love, light, joy, peace. The words were etched in stone and stained with rainbow colors. As I stood on the triumphant rock, my Father in heaven began to laugh.

Dripping in sweat, I mustered every ounce of strength to keep my feet upon the rock, perplexed by His mighty roaring laughter that seemed to shake the ground underneath my feet! In the twinkle of an eye, I could feel the strength of God surge inside my innermost being, filling me with healing rivers of rainbows and His love rushing through me.

A hearty voice chimed into the miraculous encounter, "You made it, my child. You made it through the trials, and the testing of your faith! You made it through the deadly peril and you made it through the warring with your enemies! From dooming deserts, to wavering waters, armies' attacking arrows, to confining caves and mega mountains."

"Do you see where your faith feet landed you, my chosen one?"

I looked down and saw my feet shone red, orange and gold. I trembled with the Spirit's power as I marveled that my feet were on fire with the glory of God!

"I've chosen you, my saint, my child, to carry good news to the poor, to the broken, and to the forlorn. To the orphan and the addict, to the paralyzed and lame. To carry my gospel to the very ends of the earth. Without this training you would never be strong enough. I had to teach you through every test and every trial."

> Blessed is the one who perseveres under trial because, having stood the test, that person will receive the crown of life that the Lord has promised to those who love him. (James 1:12 NIV)

"Well done, good and faithful servant. Now go feed my sheep and teach from these truths of old. Teach from these years of suffering and from your firm footing upon the rock of ages, bring many more to the top of this mountain to meet me. And at the end of your days when heaven manifests as your home, you will see all those who have followed you to me! I said it through Matthew my great evangelist,

> Therefore go and make disciples of all nations, baptizing them in the name of the Father and of the Son and of the Holy Spirit. (Matthew 28:19 NIV)

> I pray that they will all be one, just as you and I are one—as you are in me, Father, and I am in you. And may they be in us so that the world will believe you sent me. (John 17: 21 NLT)

"Oneness and overcomer." That is my claim up here on this mountain top.

I closed my eyes and treasured the beaming, bright, beautiful words of my heavenly Father. I know my call, to live for the glory of my Heavenly Father, to know Him and make Him known. I marveled at the miracles and the majesty of my Lord and Savior. By grace and through faith I carry on into my trials and tears and victory voyages over and over until I enter heaven's pearly white gates of glory!

The Giver of Life Offers Freedom

Grace supplied by our Father in Heaven, offered to each and to all who would receive the bread of life. Eat and dine, at the table in the Risen King's court. Do not let your sin hold you back from entering into the heavenlies with God. God has prepared a victorious way through the redemptive cross, and offers each and all one way up to Heaven, into a destined relationship with Him. For we all have sinned and fallen short of the glory of God (Romans 3:23). Do not wait or delay in declaring your sin, your shortcomings, your fear, your regrets, your failures, your not-yets to God. He wants to talk to you as His precious and most beloved child. God wants to whisper that your flesh is not enough and it was never designed to be enough. When sin and satan entered this world in the book of Genesis, death came upon us and we became like the curse of the fall. But God rose to life after death on a cross to pay and atone for your sin and brokenness. Rejoice! Your Father in Heaven offers you joy, salvation and blessings today. Repent and hear your Father's voice singing over you. Let your heart declare Abba Father and receive the prize of eternal life — a life of pure, all-encompassing fulfillment through the only way, truth and life Jesus, and enter into communion with the Father through the presence of the Holy Spirit!

You're invited to climb the great Mercy Mountain of God.

The Manna of Life.

The Lord is not slow in keeping his promise, as some understand slowness. Instead he is patient with you, not wanting anyone to perish, but everyone to come to repentance.

2 Peter 3:9 (NIV)

Then Jesus declared, "I am the bread of life. Whoever comes to me will never go hungry, and whoever believes in me will never be thirsty."

John 6:35 (NIV)

"The Sovereign Lord is my strength; he makes my feet like the feet of a deer, he enables me to tread on the heights."

HABAKKUK 3:19 (NIV)

www.ingramcontent.com/pod-product-compliance
Lightning Source LLC
Chambersburg PA
CBHW041455010526
44107CB00014B/1047